ASTROLOGICAL SOUL CARE

SELF-CARE RITUALS AND ROUTINES FOR THE ZODIAC SEASONS

SARA MCCORMICK

Text © 2022 Sara McCormick
Compilation, design and layout © 2022 Fox Lane Publishing
ISBN: 9798440526242

First Print: April 2022

www.soulcareastrology.com

Content

INTRODUCTION

The world around us reflects our moods, aspirations, and goals. We can see this in our desire to turn inward and rest during the winter months, just like nature goes dormant and tends to the roots below the earth. And as the world awakens in the spring, we clean our house and invite new energy in, spending more time outdoors as the days warm. But the four seasons that we're familiar with, spring, summer, winter, and autumn, aren't the only seasons we can look to for guidance. The zodiac seasons help us navigate our year as well. Zodiac seasons are month-long 'seasons' that change as the sun moves through each of the twelve zodiac signs over a year. Because our year has 365 days, the dates of the zodiac seasons aren't exactly from year to year, but they generally range from the 21st of one month to the 20th of the next, give or take a few days. We can look to the zodiac seasons as reflections of our growth throughout the year.

You'll find a journey through the zodiac seasons on the following pages, including suggestions for each, such as grounding practices, gemstone correspondences, and journal prompts.

You can also use this guide to briefly look into your Sun, Moon, or Rising sign.

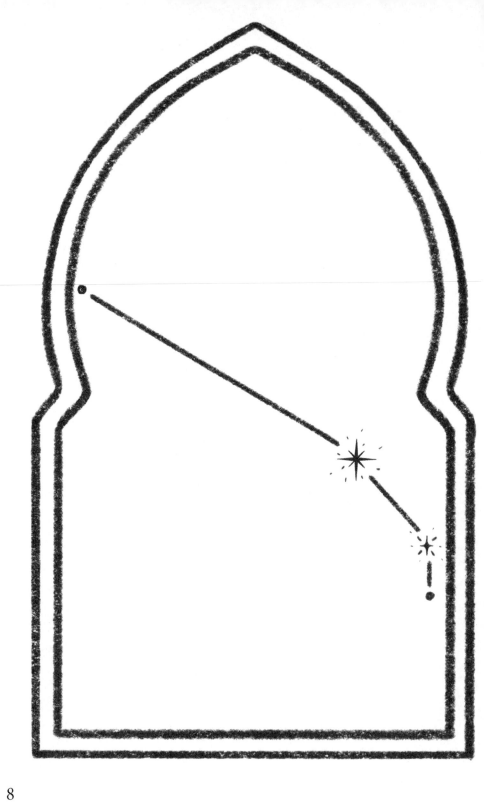

ARIES

Aries is the first sign of the zodiac, and this energy reflects that. Aries loves getting started on new ideas and being the first to finish. This sign has lots of energy and constantly seeks new inspiration to fuel its fire. The need to be independent and original is at the forefront of everything they do, and they're able to be great leaders because of this drive.

Aries is ruled by Mars, the planet of energy and willpower, and it's this energy that Aries uses to drive their focus forward. Aries folks are often naturally athletic and competitive. They don't like looking to the future but live in the present moment. Although they love starting new projects, they can have trouble focusing and finishing if there isn't something to 'win' at the end.

Aries Correspondences

House	Element	Quality	Planetary Ruler
1st	Fire	Cardinal	Mars

Season	Body Part
Spring	Head

Aries Season Energy

With Aries Season comes a fresh burst of energy for all of us, and we're ready to rush ahead, confident that we can take on the world. A good dose of Aries energy can charge us with leadership and passion. The rush that can come with this season is akin to the boom at the starting line as you take off for the race. We're ready for adventure!

IN BALANCE	OUT OF BALANCE
Assertive	Angry
Bold	Inpatient
Courageous	Immature
Ready to take action	Pushy
Leader	Domineering
Ambitious	Reckless
Independent	Reactive
Tries new things	Takes too many risks
Pioneering	Fears being trapped
Fearless	Argumentative

Soul Care Tools

The magic of Aries is that it is right at home in action. So if your Aries vibes are out of balance on either end of the spectrum, whether you're feeling not assertive enough or too demanding, you can use movement to help find that balance. A good hike or another activity of choice can help you find your center again. Some boxing might do the trick if you're looking to add a little Aries fire to your energy.

Body Awareness

Aries rules the head, so headaches can pop up when Aries energy is left to run wild. Aries tends to go full speed until something is physically in the way, like a blinding headache. Aries doesn't like to pause for too long, so it's good to schedule some quick check-ins throughout the day. A brief five meditation in the morning, another few minutes stretching at your desk at lunch, and a dance party in the evening can help you stay connected.

Herbs

Our herbal allies can also help us keep our energy more in balance. If you struggle to embody the assertive Aries fire, you may want to include some warming herbs into your diet, ginger tea or add ginger to your cooking. Or, if you find yourself a little too hot under the collar and need to slow down that impulsive or rash drive, try some Yarrow or Nettles, which are a great addition to a spring salad.

Gemstones

Gemstones are another great way to connect to the energy of the season. Perhaps not surprisingly, Fire Agate is an excellent stone for Aries Season, as it helps stoke your inner fire and boost your energy. It also acts as a shield fit for the warrior of the zodiac, keeping negative energy away as it increases your mental strength and sense of security. Red aventurine is another fiery gem that ignites your passion. Red aventurine fills you with increased desire, both in intimacy and all other areas of your life. It fuels you with the desire to take on new challenges, turn creative ideas into pursuits, and act on your intentions. Armed with additional stable Earth energies, this stone also keeps you centered.

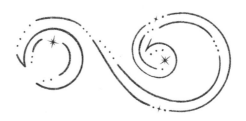

I am up for this challenge.

Nothing will stop me, and I pioneer my way.

I have confidence in myself and my inner fire.

My courage will light the way.

Journal Prompts

Where are you too focused on yourself?

_____

_____

_____

How can you use your talents and gifts to help fight and
champion others?

_____

_____

_____

What nourishes your inner sense of fire and willpower?

_____

_____

_____

Aries Season Horoscopes

Aries
You're gaining a clearer understanding of who you are as the Sun illuminates your inner rebirth. This clarity helps you take spontaneous action towards the new and exciting to carve out your path forward.

Taurus
You may feel like retreating from the world and spending time alone now. Use this time to reflect on the year past, dream of the year ahead, and refill your energetic cup.

Gemini
Your focus is shifting to your community and friends. Groups and gatherings are important to you now, and you're feeling social and lighthearted.

Cancer
Now is the best time of the year to move forward in your career. Recognition and responsibility go hand in hand as the Sun illuminates this part of your chart.

Leo
Adventure calls your name as you seek new experiences and more meaning in your life. Travel, education, learning new hobbies, and exploring your spirituality all attract your attention.

Virgo
This is a time of profound transformation, as the sun highlights your sense of personal power. The next month is great for therapy -

shadow work, and anything that helps clear the cobwebs out of the mental closet.

Libra
You'll find your power by joining with others now, both in personal and professional life. Cultivate a sense of partnership in your relationships and be open about voicing your needs.

Scorpio
The stars give you the green light to shake up your daily routine and put some nourishing practices in place. Attention to your habits now sets the foundation for your future growth in all areas of your life.

Sagittarius
You now want to stretch your legs and express yourself after sticking close to home and nesting. Creative adventures take precedence now, and you're encouraged to follow your spontaneity when it comes to playing, pleasure, and creativity.

Capricorn
Your focus turns to your home and family and creating a safe, nurturing nest to retreat to. You desire to put down roots and feel a sense of belonging. Now is a time to go inward and nourish yourself.

Aquarius
This is a time perfect for making new connections, connecting with old friends, networking, and collaborating with others. Speaking up and using your voice has a stronger impact now, and you share your message with ease.

Pisces
This is when you are focused on security, what helps you feel safe and comfortable, and what you value. If you set your mind to making a financial plan for the year ahead, you might find that it pays off later.

Aries Season Journal

What did I learn this season?

_____

_____

_____

What am I still learning?

_____

_____

_____

_____

What am I releasing?

_____

_____

_____

_____

_____

_____

What do I intend for next season?

_____

_____

_____

Any other thoughts, dreams, or desires you wish to note:

_____

_____

_____

_____

_____

_____

_____

_____

_____

_____

_____

_____

_____

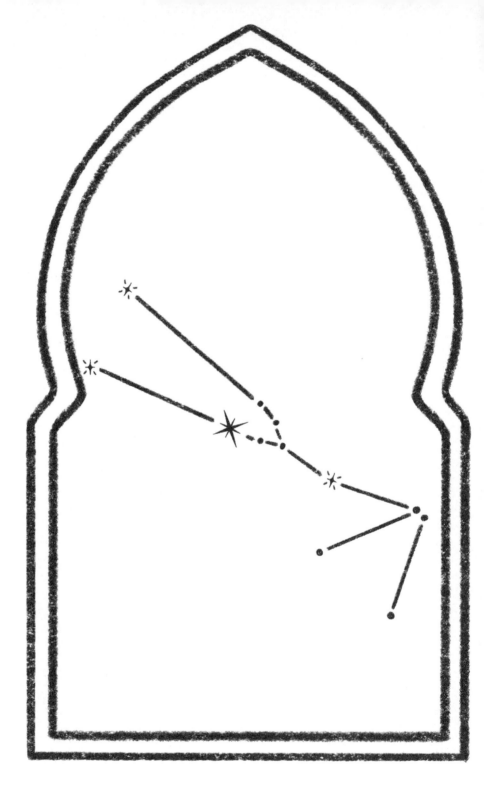

TAURUS

Taurus prefers to take their time. This sign is deeply rooted and connected to the five senses, making them sensual and pleasure-seeking. Taurus is efficient and sensible and does not rush into anything new. This sign is also a hard worker that puts in a steady effort. Taurus is ruled by Venus, the planet of love, money, and beauty, and it is this beauty that Taurus so effortlessly sees within the world around them. Like the bull they are associated with, Taurus can be stubborn as it is a fixed sign. Once its mind is made up, there is little you can do to change it. As an Earth sign, Taurus is grounded and patient and very sensual and is attracted to the more refined comforts in life. Comfort and security for Taurus come from experiencing life through the senses.

Taurus Correspondences

House	Element	Quality	Planetary Ruler
2nd	Earth	Fixed	Venus

	Season	Body Part	
	Spring	Throat	

Taurus Season Energy

For Taurus Season, we tend to feel more like slowing down, to take note of the beauty and pleasure around us. When Taurus energy is out of balance, we can feel like clinging to our possessions, materialistic and controlling. We may feel stuck in survival mode, grabbing onto anything we can reach for comfort and safety. If we're unsure or feel unready, we will stubbornly dig in our heels and resist action.

IN BALANCE	OUT OF BALANCE
Patient	Materialistic
Grounded	Stubborn
Slowing down	Lazy
Enjoys life	Overindulgent
Sensual	Controlling
Dependable	Survival mode
Determined	Inflexible
Peaceful	Greedy
Conservative	Possessive
Reliable	Predictable

Soul Care Tools

If you feel that your Taurus energy is out of balance, the key is grounding and leaning more into the trust that you are safe and secure, the crux of feelings that tend to spur out of balance Taurus energy. Grounding exercise and medications can help. Spending time in nature can be beneficial. Working on your trust muscles can help - try journaling to talking with a friend to lessen your worries. Even though Taurus is a strong and dependable bull, you don't have to carry all of the weight alone. You may find comfort in tapping into that Taurus energy by bringing more comfort and beauty into your home. Try carving out a sacred space for yourself with objects that will soothe your senses.

Body Awareness

Taurus rules the neck and ears so that tension can form in these areas. This also includes the throat and our ability to use our voice. With Taurus energy, we need to feel comfortable expressing our thoughts. Even though Taurus is an Earth sign and not a Water sign, it is very sensual, and therefore it is very sensitive.

Herbs

Our herbal allies can also help us keep our energy more in balance. If you find yourself struggling to embody the patient and persistent Taurus energy, you may want to include some herbs such as rose or violet in your day - both work well in teas! Or you could have them in a bath or luxurious facial steam. A Taurus treat, to be sure!

Gemstones

Gemstones are another great way to connect to the energy of the season. Malachite is a wonderful gemstone to work with for Taurus energy as it helps protect you from negative energies, as well as electromagnetic frequency protection. It is also said to help carry energy for you so you can more easily move through difficult times in your life with stamina and perseverance, two noble qualities of Taurus energy.

Pyrite is another wonderful Taurus season gemstone, as it is said to help attract financial abundance and prosperity to you. Taurus is one of the zodiac signs that deals with finances, and this energy can help you build a solid foundation for your financial future.

Affirmations

Beauty can be fragile and strong.

I am leaning into trust.

I deserve a luxurious life.

I am creating financial independence in a joyful way.

 # Journal Prompts

What helps you feel grounded and secure?

_____

_____

_____

Is there a part of nature that helps you relax and slow down?

_____

_____

_____

What do you find beautiful and soothing?

_____

_____

_____

Taurus Season Horoscopes

Aries
This is when you are focused on security, what helps you feel safe and comfortable, and what you value. If you set your mind to making a financial plan for the year ahead, you might find that it pays off later.

Taurus
You're gaining a clearer understanding of who you are as the Sun illuminates your inner rebirth. This clarity helps you take spontaneous action towards the new and exciting to carve out your path forward.

Gemini
You may feel like retreating from the world and spending time alone now. Use this time to reflect on the year past, dream of the year ahead, and refill your energetic cup.

Cancer
Your focus is shifting to your community and friends. Groups and gatherings are important to you now, and you're feeling social and lighthearted.

Leo
Now is the best time of the year to move forward in your career. Recognition and responsibility go hand in hand as the Sun illuminates this part of your chart.

Virgo
Adventure calls your name as you seek new experiences and more meaning in your life. Travel, education, learning new hobbies, and exploring your spirituality all attract your attention.

Libra
This is a time of profound transformation, as the sun highlights your sense of personal power. The next month is great for therapy shadow work, and anything that helps clear the cobwebs out of the mental closet.

Scorpio
You'll find your power by joining with others now, both in personal and professional life. Cultivate a sense of partnership in your relationships and be open about voicing your needs.

Sagittarius
The stars give you the green light to shake up your daily routine and put some nourishing practices in place. Attention to your habits now sets the foundation for your future growth in all areas of your life.

Capricorn
You now want to stretch your legs and express yourself after sticking close to home and nesting. Creative adventures take precedence now, and you're encouraged to follow your spontaneity when it comes to playing, pleasure, and creativity.

Aquarius
Your focus turns to your home and family and creating a safe, nurturing nest to retreat to. You desire to put down roots and feel a sense of belonging. Now is a time to go inward and nourish yourself.

Pisces
This is a time perfect for making new connections, connecting with old friends, networking, and collaborating with others. Speaking up and using your voice has a stronger impact now, and you share your message with ease.

Taurus Season Journal

What did I learn this season?

_____

_____

_____

What am I still learning?

_____

_____

_____

What am I releasing?

_____

_____

_____

_____

_____

_____

What do I intend for next season?

_____

_____

_____

Any other thoughts, dreams, or desires you wish to note:

_____

_____

_____

_____

_____

_____

_____

_____

_____

_____

_____

_____

_____

_____

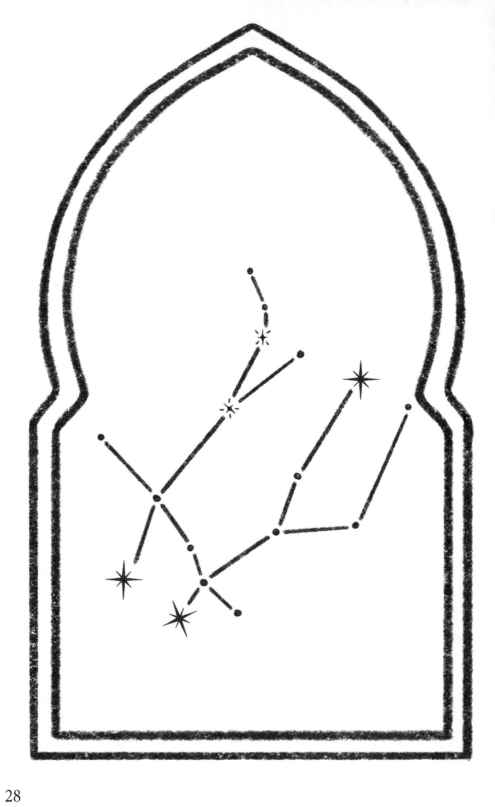

GEMINI

Gemini continuously seeks out new information and then looks for others to share it with. Gemini naturally needs to be able to express themselves, and their curious nature keeps them adapting and shape-shifting to the world around them. This can make it hard for those close to them to feel like they know them. Gemini's are creative, flexible, clever, sociable, networking and conversing easily. Gemini is ruled by Mercury, the planet of communication, technology, and how we think. This is why Gemini is such a master of the mind, able to quickly understand concepts and communicate promptly and succinctly, whether in writing or speaking. Gemini can often excel at multitasking and need the mental stimulation of juggling various tasks at once.

Gemini Correspondences

House	Element	Quality	Planetary Ruler
3rd	Air	Mutable	Mercury

Season	Body Part
Spring	Nervous System

Gemini Season Energy

For Gemini Season, the focus shifts to connection, community, and communication. Gemini is curious and playful and loves gathering information to share with others. When Gemini energy is out of balance, our energy can feel scattered and restless. We have trouble focusing, making decisions, and connecting to our body.

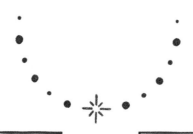

IN BALANCE	OUT OF BALANCE
Curious	Restless
Childlike	Indecisive
Flexible	Scattered
Open-minded	Distracted
Communicative	Superficial
Mobile	Gossips
Fun-loving	In the head
On the move	Mischievous
Expressive	Cheater
Social	Disconnected

Soul Care Tools

Gemini season calls us to evaluate how we communicate. If we talk more than we listen or are prone to gossip and spreading misinformation, Gemini season may challenge us to slow down and listen more. If we're hesitant or afraid to speak up and share what is on our minds, we may be called to step up and use our voice. It's all about finding the balance between the two. Gemini is often seen as the communicator of the zodiac, but it is essential to remember that communicating is about more than just talking and chatting away. It is just as important to actively listen with empathy and a compassionate heart. We also have to keep in mind that how we speak to and about ourselves has just as much power as our words to talk about others.

Body Awareness

Gemini rules the nervous system, which is seen in the restless, scattered, anxious, and downright nervous energy we can feel when our Gemini energy is out of balance. Meditation is vital for soothing our nervous system.

Herbs

Our herbal allies can also help us keep our energy more in balance. If you feel pulled in multiple directions, Peppermint is a beautiful herb for focusing on one task at a time. You can diffuse peppermint essential oil in your diffuser or drink peppermint tea. Be cautious of using peppermint oil on your skin, as it is irritates if not diluted properly. If you feel the urge to rush ahead, to be first to cross the finish line and stand in the spotlight, try diffusing some lavender during meditation or just rest to help you slow down and connect back to your body.

Gemstones

Gemstones are another great way to connect to the energy of the season. Even though Gemini loves to chat, sometimes we can fear our emotions during this season. Orange Calcite helps us recognize and accept our feelings instead of trying to tune them out and chatter over them.

Serpentine is lovely for grounding and getting clarity, especially if you're having trouble seeing the forest for the trees. Sometimes there is so much input that we are overwhelmed with choices, and this stone helps to soothe that.

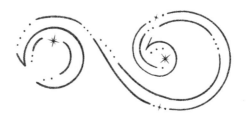 Affirmations

My words are abundantly flowing.

I am speaking with clarity.

I honor my duality.

 Journal Prompts

How can you be more flexible and adaptable?

_____

_____

_____

Where do you need to focus your communications?

_____

_____

_____

What helps you stay focused?

_____

_____

_____

Gemini Season Horoscopes

Aries
This is a time perfect for making new connections, connecting with old friends, networking, and collaborating with others. Speaking up and using your voice has a stronger impact now, and you share your message with ease.

Taurus
This is when you are focused on security, what helps you feel safe and comfortable, and what you value. If you set your mind to making a financial plan for the year ahead, you might find that it pays off later.

Gemini
You're gaining a clearer understanding of who you are as the Sun illuminates your inner rebirth. This clarity helps you take spontaneous action towards the new and exciting to carve out your path forward.

Cancer
You may feel like retreating from the world and spending time alone now. Use this time to reflect on the year past, dream of the year ahead, and refill your energetic cup.

Leo
Your focus is shifting to your community and friends. Groups and gatherings are important to you now, and you're feeling social and lighthearted.

Virgo
Now is the best time of the year to move forward in your career. Recognition and responsibility go hand in hand as the Sun illuminates this part of your chart.

Libra
Adventure calls your name as you seek new experiences and more meaning in your life. Travel, education, learning new hobbies, and exploring your spirituality all attract your attention.

Scorpio
This is a time of profound transformation, as the sun highlights your sense of personal power. The next month is great for therapy shadow work, and anything that helps clear the cobwebs out of the mental closet.

Sagittarius
You'll find your power by joining with others now, both in personal and professional life. Cultivate a sense of partnership in your relationships and be open about voicing your needs.

Capricorn
The stars give you the green light to shake up your daily routine and put some nourishing practices in place. Attention to your habits now sets the foundation for your future growth in all areas of your life.

Aquarius
You now want to stretch your legs and express yourself after sticking close to home and nesting. Creative adventures take precedence now, and you're encouraged to follow your spontaneity when it comes to playing, pleasure, and creativity.

Pisces
Your focus turns to your home and family and creating a safe, nurturing nest to retreat to. You desire to put down roots and feel a sense of belonging. Now is a time to go inward and nourish yourself.

Gemini Season Journal

What did I learn this season?

_____

_____

_____

What am I still learning?

_____

_____

_____

What am I releasing?

_____

_____

_____

_____

_____

What do I intend for next season?

_____

_____

_____

Any other thoughts, dreams, or desires you wish to note:

_____

_____

_____

_____

_____

_____

_____

_____

_____

_____

_____

_____

_____

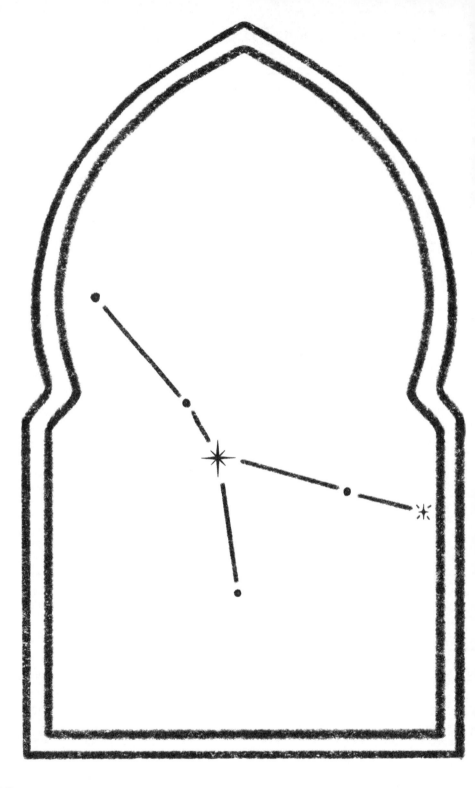

CANCER

Cancer is focused on the home. Think for a moment about the archetype of Cancer, the crab. In a way, the crab carries its home, or shelter, with it. When it is startled or frightened, it can quickly retreat into the safety of its shell. Cancer is similar, with a strong survival instinct that is very protective of themselves and those they care about. Cancer doesn't open up quickly and can hide behind a tough exterior. Because of this, they can become very defensive if they feel threatened. Cancer is ruled by the Moon, while not a planet, it is a luminary and reflects our inner landscape, or emotions, back to us. This is why Cancer is such a highly intuitive and sympathetic sign, in touch with their feelings and the emotions of those around them.

Cancer Correspondences

House	Element	Quality	Planetary Ruler
4th	Water	Cardinal	Moon

Season	Body Part
Summer	Chest, stomach

Cancer Season Energy

For Cancer Season, we turn to themes of family, safety, home, comfort, and nurturing others. Cancer loves to see its family thrive and grow. They go out of their way to support and nurture those they love. Safety is paramount, and Cancer often needs to feel like home is a haven, a place to retreat to when the outside world becomes too much.

IN BALANCE	OUT OF BALANCE
Homebody	Moody
Sensitive	Reactive
Emotional	Dependent
Receptive	Lazy
Nurturing	Possessive
Sympathetic	Clingy
Intuitive	Needy
Supportive	Fearful
Protective	Irritable
Domestic	Manipulative

Soul Care Tools

Cancer needs to feel safe and secure to focus on nurturing themselves and not just those around them. Creating a relaxing space within your home to retreat to when you feel overwhelmed, and reactive is necessary. Dive deep into what feels good and helps you relax for what you include in your space. You may find yourself drawn to specific colors or textures that you want to incorporate, or perhaps you have a favorite piece of artwork that soothes your soul every time you look at it.

Body Awareness

Cancer rules the breasts and stomach, and the watery, changeable nature of Cancer can impact our stomach and how it feels. But this also applies to where many of us feel our intuition: our stomach. The saying trust your gut is perfect for Cancer season. Perhaps you feel a tightness in your belly when your intuition tells you no, or a fluttering excitement when she says yes. Take note and listen to what your body tells you.

Herbs

Our herbal allies can help us keep our energy in balance. If you feel anxious and worried about the future, Aloe Vera is a fantastic herb to help you to stay in the present. Keeping an Aloe Vera plant in your space helps purify the air, but you can also use the gel within the plant to make a soothing face mask. You can purchase Aloe Vera juice to drink! If you find your tummy giving your trouble during Cancer Season, Chamomile is the herb of choice to soothe your digestive tract. You can purchase Chamomile tea at many local grocery stores, but you can also make it yourself if you have a Chamomile plant that you are growing.

Gemstones

Gemstones are another great way to connect to the energy of the season. Known to many as the birthstone of Cancer, Moonstone is the stone of the Moon, the planetary ruler of Cancer. Just as the moon goes through phases, so does Cancer, and Moonstone helps you attune to those phases, knowing when to act and when to let go and rest.

Opal helps you let go of things that are no longer serving you, so you can focus on what does help you flourish and grow. Opal is excellent for releasing old programs, behaviors, and patterns that hold us back.

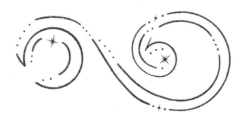

Affirmations

I let my emotions flow through me.

I trust my intuition.

I can retreat to safety when I need to.

 # Journal Prompts

What do you need to feel safe and secure?

_____

_____

_____

How can you nurture yourself?

_____

_____

_____

What helps connect you to your intuition?

_____

_____

_____

Cancer Season Horoscopes

Aries
Your focus turns to your home and family and creating a safe, nurturing nest to retreat to. You desire to put down roots and feel a sense of belonging. Now is a time to go inward and nourish yourself.

Taurus
This is a time perfect for making new connections, connecting with old friends, networking, and collaborating with others. Speaking up and using your voice has a stronger impact now, and you share your message with ease.

Gemini
This is when you are focused on security, what helps you feel safe and comfortable, and what you value. If you set your mind to making a financial plan for the year ahead, you might find that it pays off later.

Cancer
You're gaining a clearer understanding of who you are as the Sun illuminates your inner rebirth. This clarity helps you take spontaneous action towards the new and exciting to carve out your path forward.

Leo
You may feel like retreating from the world and spending time alone now. Use this time to reflect on the year past, dream of the year ahead, and refill your energetic cup.

Virgo

Your focus is shifting to your community and friends. Groups and gatherings are important to you now, and you're feeling social and lighthearted.

Libra

Now is the best time of the year to move forward in your career. Recognition and responsibility go hand in hand as the Sun illuminates this part of your chart.

Scorpio

Adventure calls your name as you seek new experiences and more meaning in your life. Travel, education, learning new hobbies, and exploring your spirituality all attract your attention.

Sagittarius

This is a time of profound transformation, as the sun highlights your sense of personal power. The next month is great for therapy shadow work, and anything that helps clear the cobwebs out of the mental closet.

Capricorn

You'll find your power by joining with others now, both in personal and professional life. Cultivate a sense of partnership in your relationships and be open about voicing your needs.

Aquarius

The stars give you the green light to shake up your daily routine and put some nourishing practices in place. Attention to your habits now sets the foundation for your future growth in all areas of your life.

Pisces

You now want to stretch your legs and express yourself after sticking close to home and nesting. Creative adventures take precedence now, and you're encouraged to follow your spontaneity when it comes to playing, pleasure, and creativity.

Cancer Season Journal

What did I learn this season?

_____

_____

_____

What am I still learning?

_____

_____

_____

_____

What am I releasing?

_____

_____

_____

_____

_____

What do I intend for next season?

_____

_____

_____

Any other thoughts, dreams, or desires you wish to note:

_____

_____

_____

_____

_____

_____

_____

_____

_____

_____

_____

_____

_____

_____

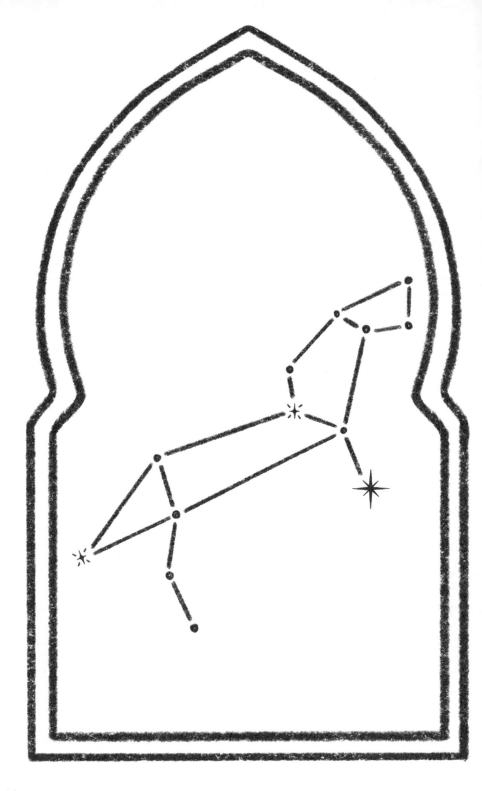

LEO

Leo is the bold leader in the limelight. Where the leadership of Aries stems from wanting to be the first, Leo likes to bask in the spotlight and glow of admiration. Leo's can be a great inspiration, and the life of the party, and they're not afraid to be confident in themselves and what they bring to the table. They have a regal and dignified air about them, which sometimes comes across as ego. Leo is ruled by the Sun, and just like their ruler, they aren't afraid to shine. The Sun represents your fullest expression and potential in astrology, and Leo has no fear of being who they are. This passionate sign plays and works hard and rules with their heart.

Leo Correspondences

House	Element	Quality	Planetary Ruler
5th	Fire	Fixed	Sun

Season	Body Part
Summer	Heart, spine

# Leo Season Energy

For Leo Season, we turn to themes of creativity, playfulness, and pride. The symbol for Leo, the lion, is the perfect archetype for this sign. Proud, regal, warm, powerful, playful, and charismatic, the lion is a creature we're all fascinated with from the moment we see him. Leo is the same, with a magnetism we're drawn to like a moth to a flame.

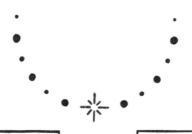

IN BALANCE	OUT OF BALANCE
Loving	Narcissistic
Creative	Snobby
Passionate	Drama queen
Confident	Arrogant
Generous	Cruel
Playful	Dominating
Noble	Stubborn
Affectionate	Attention seeking
Charismatic	Self-centered
Warm	Autocratic

Soul Care Tools

Not surprisingly, since Leo is a fire sign, Leo season occurs during the peak of Summer in the northern hemisphere when the Sun is at its strongest and brightest. Leo is rejuvenated by the Sun and often will seek out its warmth, much like a cat, to recharge. One of the significant symbols of a lion, the mane, is also a symbol that Leo takes pride in. It's not uncommon for a Leo to take extra care of their hair and prioritize it as part of their self-care routine.

Body Awareness

Leo rules the spine and heart, so connecting with our heart space and knowing if we're moving too quickly or too slowly is essential. Moving your body so your spine stays flexible is vital for staying open during this time.

Herbs

The herbal allies for Leo boost the fiery, optimistic nature, such as Sunflower, and those that help soothe the inner fires when they burn too brightly, such as Hawthorn. If you're feeling like the heat of Leo has become too much for you, and anxiety and restlessness are settling in, Hawthorn helps slow the body down. It's also an excellent herb for nourishing the heart, one of the areas that Leo rules. If you find yourself on the other side of the spectrum and need some help stoking your inner fire, the Sunflower flower essence can help you radiate energy with warmth and confidence.

Gemstones

Gemstones are another great way to connect to the energy of the season. Yellow Jasper is fantastic for protection (especially when traveling) but also helps encourage creativity, courage, and vitality - all themes of Leo Season!

Tangerine Quartz is a quartz that forms where there is a water cavity with a high Hematite content - which creates the rust that colors the quartz. This gemstone helps raise your vibration and live in the present, making you more present and playful.

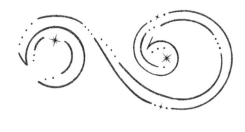

Affirmations

I take pride in my joy and creativity.

I claim my crown and sovereign starlight.

I am worthy of taking up space.

Journal Prompts

What about yourself are you proud of?

_____

_____

_____

Are there times when your ego gets the best of you?

_____

_____

_____

How do you incorporate play into your day?

_____

_____

_____

Leo Season Horoscopes

Aries
You now want to stretch your legs and express yourself after sticking close to home and nesting. Creative adventures take precedence now, and you're encouraged to follow your spontaneity when it comes to playing, pleasure, and creativity.

Taurus
Your focus turns to your home and family and creating a safe, nurturing nest to retreat to. You desire to put down roots and feel a sense of belonging. Now is a time to go inward and nourish yourself.

Gemini
This is a time perfect for making new connections, connecting with old friends, networking, and collaborating with others. Speaking up and using your voice has a stronger impact now, and you share your message with ease.

Cancer
This is when you are focused on security, what helps you feel safe and comfortable, and what you value. If you set your mind to making a financial plan for the year ahead, you might find that it pays off later.

Leo
You're gaining a clearer understanding of who you are as the Sun illuminates your inner rebirth. This clarity helps you take spontaneous action towards the new and exciting to carve out your path forward.

Virgo
You may feel like retreating from the world and spending time alone now. Use this time to reflect on the year past, dream of the year ahead, and refill your energetic cup.

Libra
Your focus is shifting to your community and friends. Groups and gatherings are important to you now, and you're feeling social and lighthearted.

Scorpio
Now is the best time of the year to move forward in your career. Recognition and responsibility go hand in hand as the Sun illuminates this part of your chart.

Sagittarius
Adventure calls your name as you seek new experiences and more meaning in your life. Travel, education, learning new hobbies, and exploring your spirituality all attract your attention.

Capricorn
This is a time of profound transformation, as the sun highlights your sense of personal power. The next month is great for therapy shadow work, and anything that helps clear the cobwebs out of the mental closet.

Aquarius
You'll find your power by joining with others now, both in personal and professional life. Cultivate a sense of partnership in your relationships and be open about voicing your needs.

Pisces
The stars give you the green light to shake up your daily routine and put some nourishing practices in place. Attention to your habits now sets the foundation for your future growth in all areas of your life.

Leo Season Journal

What did I learn this season?

_____

_____

_____

What am I still learning?

_____

_____

_____

What am I releasing?

_____

_____

_____

_____

_____

What do I intend for next season?

_____

_____

_____

Any other thoughts, dreams, or desires you wish to note:

_____

_____

_____

_____

_____

_____

_____

_____

_____

_____

_____

_____

_____

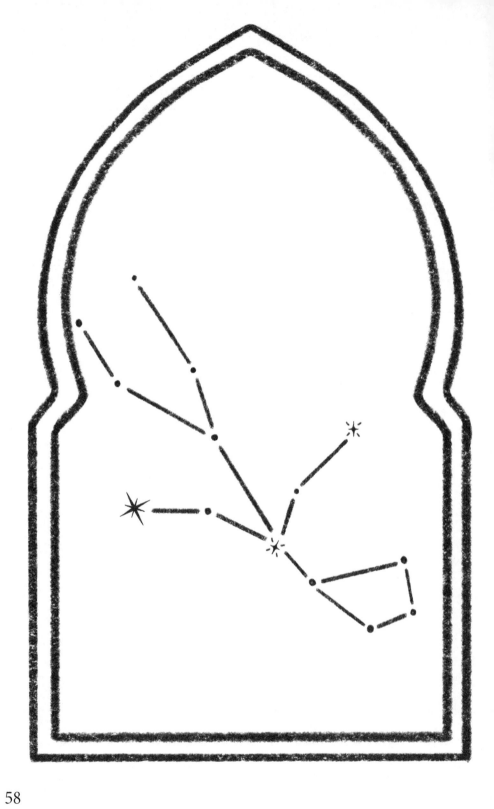

VIRGO

While Leo likes to be center stage, Virgo prefers to work behind the scenes. As a mutable earth sign, Virgo is practical and analytical. The symbol for Virgo is often misunderstood, with the focus being on the idea of Virgo being a virgin, but the reality is that Virgo is a maiden carrying sheaves of wheat from the harvest. Virgo has the skill and discernment to separate the wheat from the chaff, which is not something everyone can do. Virgo is ruled by Mercury, the planet of communication, the mind, and technology. Virgo excels at critical thinking and seeing the fine details that others might miss.

Virgo Correspondences

House	Element	Quality	Planetary Ruler
6th	Earth	Mutable	Mercury

Season	Body Part
Summer	Digestive system

Virgo Season Energy

For Virgo Season, we turn to themes of healing, critical thinking, and service to others. Astrologically Virgo season is the last month of summer when many crops flourish, and Virgo's critical eye helps separate the wheat from the shaft, knowing what is valuable. Virgo is in harmony with the world around them when using this analytical mind for service to others, and things flow. But when out of balance, Virgo energy tends towards overly critical and repressed.

IN BALANCE	OUT OF BALANCE
Practical	Shy
Healer	Worries too much
Discerning	Hypochondriac
Meticulous	Overly critical
Modest	Perfectionist
Precise	Self-deprecating
Health-conscious	Repressed
Dutiful	Overly conservative
Analytical	Neurotic
Efficient	Uptight

Soul Care Tools

Virgo is ruled by Mercury and has a quick mind ready, and can make connections and judgments as fast as the information flows to them. So in Virgo season, we can find ourselves with more mental restlessness and overall nervous energy to deal with. The gentle movement of the body, talking with others, and working with plants and herbs help ground Virgo energy into something more practical and holistic.

Body Awareness

Virgo rules the intestines, which research has significantly shown impacts our mental alertness and mood. The ease with which our gut absorbs nutrients from our food directly correlates with our serotonin levels and spirit, so keeping our colon healthy impacts all the other parts of our body! A fiber-rich diet can go a long way with this, and probiotics can also help.

Herbs

The herbal allies for Virgo help soothe the gut and the mind, which are more connected than we realize. Fennel is a great digestive aid as a tea, gentle enough for use after a heavy meal, and are strong enough for soothing more chronic inflammation. When it comes to a nervous or anxious mind, Lavender is an excellent herbal ally. You can take lavender internally as a tea or tincture or use Lavender essential oil in your diffuser or your bath salts. This floral aroma will help soothe your worried mind so you can ground and find your center once again.

Gemstones

Gemstones are another great way to connect to the energy of the season. Since Mercury rules Virgo, we can become stuck in our minds during Virgo Season. Moss Agate helps us reconnect to our body and emotions through gentle grounding.

Peridot is one of the best gemstones for sharpening your perception and analytical eye, a must for Virgo Season. A bonus? It also helps to release old baggage and emotional wounds and helps relax some of that well-known Virgo criticism to be kinder to yourself.

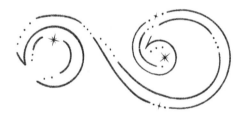

Affirmations

Purpose not perfection.

I am grounded by my routine.

I am valued for more than my work.

 Journal Prompts

What about yourself are you proud of?

_____

_____

_____

Are there times when your ego gets the best of you?

_____

_____

_____

How do you incorporate play into your day?

_____

_____

_____

Virgo Season Horoscopes

Aries
The stars give you the green light to shake up your daily routine and put some nourishing practices in place. Attention to your habits now sets the foundation for your future growth in all areas of your life.

Taurus
You now want to stretch your legs and express yourself after sticking close to home and nesting. Creative adventures take precedence now, and you're encouraged to follow your spontaneity when it comes to playing, pleasure, and creativity.

Gemini
Your focus turns to your home and family and creating a safe, nurturing nest to retreat to. You desire to put down roots and feel a sense of belonging. Now is a time to go inward and nourish yourself.

Cancer
This is a time perfect for making new connections, connecting with old friends, networking, and collaborating with others. Speaking up and using your voice has a stronger impact now, and you share your message with ease.

Leo
This is when you are focused on security, what helps you feel safe and comfortable, and what you value. If you set your mind to making a financial plan for the year ahead, you might find that it pays off later.

Virgo
You're gaining a clearer understanding of who you are as the Sun illuminates your inner rebirth. This clarity helps you take spontaneous action towards the new and exciting to carve out your path forward.

Libra
You may feel like retreating from the world and spending time alone now. Use this time to reflect on the year past, dream of the year ahead, and refill your energetic cup.

Scorpio
Your focus is shifting to your community and friends. Groups and gatherings are important to you now, and you're feeling social and lighthearted.

Sagittarius
Now is the best time of the year to move forward in your career. Recognition and responsibility go hand in hand as the Sun illuminates this part of your chart.

Capricorn
Adventure calls your name as you seek new experiences and more meaning in your life. Travel, education, learning new hobbies, and exploring your spirituality all attract your attention.

Aquarius
This is a time of profound transformation, as the sun highlights your sense of personal power. The next month is great for therapy shadow work, and anything that helps clear the cobwebs out of the mental closet.

Pisces
You'll find your power by joining with others now, both in personal and professional life. Cultivate a sense of partnership in your relationships and be open about voicing your needs.

Virgo Season Journal

What did I learn this season?

_____

_____

_____

What am I still learning?

_____

_____

_____

_____

What am I releasing?

_____

_____

_____

_____

_____

_____

What do I intend for next season?

_____

_____

_____

Any other thoughts, dreams, or desires you wish to note:

_____

_____

_____

_____

_____

_____

_____

_____

_____

_____

_____

_____

_____

_____

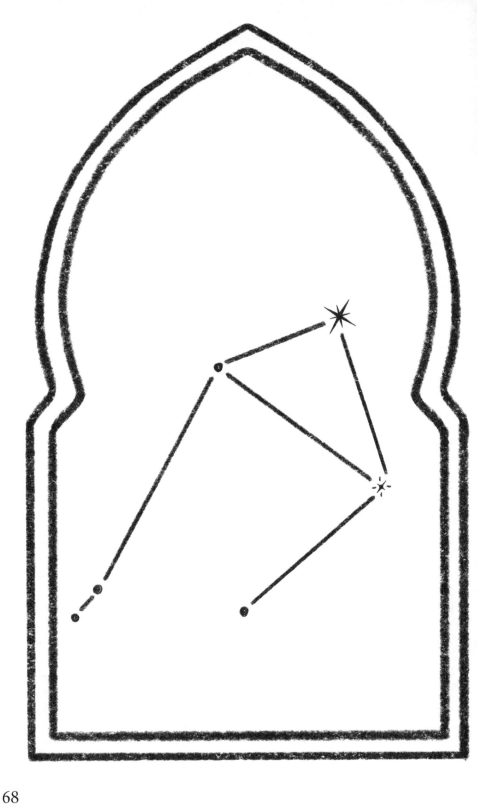

LIBRA

Libra is a cultivator of beauty and harmony. They're naturally charismatic and quickly build harmonious relationships with others. This friendly sign is cooperative but sometimes avoids speaking up in fear of rocking the boat. Part of the lesson of Libra Season is to find their balance of holding your boundaries. Libra is ruled by Venus, the planet of love, money, and beauty. This is reflected in the values of Libra, who can often see both sides of an argument or position. They seek to find justice and fairness in the world, creating harmony and balance around them.

Libra Correspondences

House	Element	Quality	Planetary Ruler
7th	Air	Cardinal	Venus

Season	Body Part
Autumn	Kidneys, skin

Libra Season Energy

For Libra Season, our focus shifts to partnerships and how we maintain our boundaries and sense of ourselves within those relationships. The beauty of Libra energy is that it allows us to see both sides of the coin and understand everyone's point of view. The downside of Libra energy is that we are so caught up in all the possibilities of everyone else's point of view that we can forget to take note of our own. Our voice gets drowned out in the sea of others.

IN BALANCE

Creates balance
Peaceful
Cooperation
Seeks to understand
Graceful
Justice
Tactful
Artistic
Sophisticated

OUT OF BALANCE

Codependent
People pleasing
Overly idealistic
Materialistic
Indecisive
Passive
Deceptive
Superficial
Resentment

Soul Care Tools

As an air sign, Libra takes the knowledge and information from the world around them and assimilates it, making swift judgment calls that allow for balance and keeping the peace, avoiding conflict if possible. This can lead to anticipating others' needs and developing codependent relationships, so firm boundaries are a must. Ruled by Venus, Libra likes to be surrounded by beauty, so self-care practices that add a touch of beauty are very much in line with Libra thinking, such as a midday break to walk among fresh flowers.

Body Awareness

Libra rules the kidneys, so drinking plenty of water is vital. The kidneys are the great cleaners of the body, helping us get rid of toxins.

Herbs

The herbal allies for Libra help keep the body in balance. Violet is not only a beautiful flower (it looks great on salads!), but it also helps support the cleansing and balancing functions of the kidneys. As an air sign, Libra can find its mind racing at night. Passionflower is a relaxing herb that helps settle the nerves, soothe the mind at bedtime, and makes a beautiful evening tea.

Gemstones

Gemstones are another great way to connect to the energy of the season. One of the things that can become a struggle during Libra Season is keeping the separation between 'me' and 'you' - the lines can become blurred and lead to codependent relationships. Blue Calcite helps you keep yourself in focus.

Aquamarine helps you feel at ease no matter your surroundings. If your inner waters are easily tossed and troubled like an ocean sea during a storm, this stone can help you keep your balance.

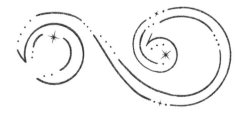 Affirmations

I bring balance to my environment.

I see the beauty around me.

I am making the best decision for me.

 *Journal Prompts*

What in your life is out of balance?

_____

_____

_____

What can you do to help correct that balance?

_____

_____

_____

What relationship needs tending now?

_____

_____

_____

Libra Season Horoscopes

Aries
You'll find your power by joining with others now, both in personal and professional life. Cultivate a sense of partnership in your relationships and be open about voicing your needs.

Taurus
The stars give you the green light to shake up your daily routine and put some nourishing practices in place. Attention to your habits now sets the foundation for your future growth in all areas of your life.

Gemini
You now want to stretch your legs and express yourself after sticking close to home and nesting. Creative adventures take precedence now, and you're encouraged to follow your spontaneity when it comes to playing, pleasure, and creativity.

Cancer
Your focus turns to your home and family and creating a safe, nurturing nest to retreat to. You desire to put down roots and feel a sense of belonging. Now is a time to go inward and nourish yourself.

Leo
This is a time perfect for making new connections, connecting with old friends, networking, and collaborating with others. Speaking up and using your voice has a stronger impact now, and you share your message with ease.

Virgo
This is when you are focused on security, what helps you feel safe and comfortable, and what you value. If you set your mind to making a financial plan for the year ahead, you might find that it pays off later.

Libra
You're gaining a clearer understanding of who you are as the Sun illuminates your inner rebirth. This clarity helps you take spontaneous action towards the new and exciting to carve out your path forward.

Scorpio
You may feel like retreating from the world and spending time alone now. Use this time to reflect on the year past, dream of the year ahead, and refill your energetic cup.

Sagittarius
Your focus is shifting to your community and friends. Groups and gatherings are important to you now, and you're feeling social and lighthearted.

Capricorn
Now is the best time of the year to move forward in your career. Recognition and responsibility go hand in hand as the Sun illuminates this part of your chart.

Aquarius
Adventure calls your name as you seek new experiences and more meaning in your life. Travel, education, learning new hobbies, and exploring your spirituality all attract your attention.

Pisces
This is a time of profound transformation, as the sun highlights your sense of personal power. The next month is great for therapy shadow work, and anything that helps clear the cobwebs out of the mental closet.

Libra Season Journal

What did I learn this season?

_____

_____

_____

What am I still learning?

_____

_____

_____

What am I releasing?

_____

_____

_____

_____

_____

What do I intend for next season?

_____

_____

_____

Any other thoughts, dreams, or desires you wish to note:

_____

_____

_____

_____

_____

_____

_____

_____

_____

_____

_____

_____

_____

_____

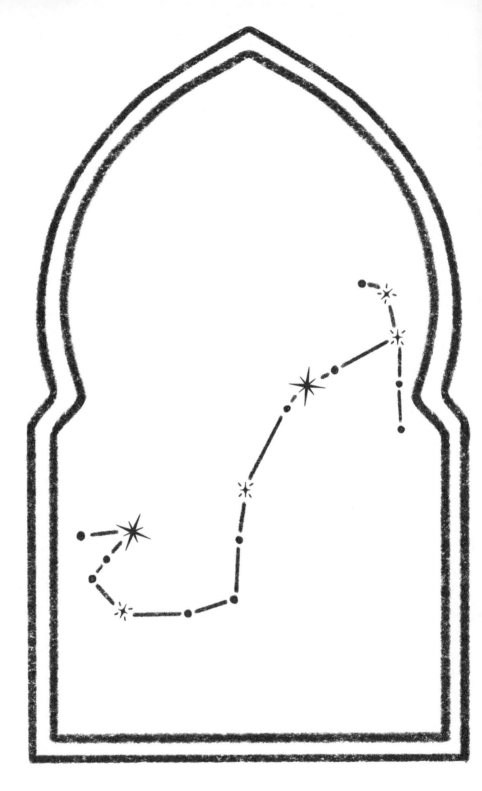

SCORPIO

Scorpio isn't afraid to face its shadow side and even embrace it. Scorpio can see past the surface layer and unearth the truth hidden behind our deepest desires. Scorpio is ruled by Pluto, the planet of transformation and breakthroughs. Scorpios often experience significant life changes or traumatic events that push them to evolve and change, learning more about who they are and being a better person from learning through experience. For Scorpio Season, we as a collective learn more about the shadow side of our nature, and things from our past that we regret may come to the surface for us to learn from them.

Scorpio Correspondences

House	Element	Quality	Planetary Ruler
8th	Water	Fixed	Mars, Pluto

Season	Body Part
Autumn	Reproductive system

Scorpio Season Energy

For Scorpio Season, our focus shifts to diving deep into our emotions and uncovering the motivation we try to keep hidden behind our actions. As a water sign, Scorpio feels very deeply, and because it is a fixed sign, it can get stuck in black and white thinking if not mindful. As much as Scorpio is comfortable diving into its depths of feelings, it sometimes forgets to look past the surface when it comes to others, reacting on instinct and first glance with suspicion or jealousy.

IN BALANCE	OUT OF BALANCE
Powerful	Black or white ideas
Passionate	Suspicious
Intense	Sarcastic
Psychological	Compulsive
Into the occult	Obsessive
Psychic	Vindictive
Magical	Unforgiving
Transformation	Secretive
Sexual	Controlling

Soul Care Tools

Scorpio energy is fantastic for helping us get in touch with the parts of ourselves we like to keep locked away or hidden. Scorpio isn't afraid to face our shadow side and even embrace it. Scorpio can see past the surface layer and unearth the truth hidden behind our deepest desires.

Body Awareness

Scorpio rules the reproductive system and organs of elimination. Scorpio can see so much around it because it absorbs information, both seen and unseen, like a sponge. This can lead to a toxic internal environment of too many feelings, sensations, and other people's energy swirling around. And like any good scorpion would, Scorpio tends to lash out when things get to this point. Sometimes Scorpio needs to step away and stop trying to figure everyone out and instead spend time alone, giving the body space to eliminate the excess energy.

Herbs

The herbal allies for Scorpio help keep this energy in balance. Holly is a natural ally when balancing the intensity of emotion that Scorpio travels through life with. The Holly flower essence is a safe and gentle way to work with this herb for balancing your energetic and emotional body. If you're feeling highly reactive and like your energy has been muddled with others, Blessed Thistle is a herb that helps settle the nerves and gently detox the body. Blessed Thistle can be worked with as a tea and is generally considered a safer option than Milk Thistle, which may pose an allergy problem to some.

Gemstones

Gemstones are another great way to connect to the energy of the season. We can seem serious on the outside, but we are swirling with feelings. Smoky Quartz can help you sort through your emotions and determine which ones are of value and which ones are holding you back. Smoky Quartz can also help you transform old emotions and experiences so that you no longer carry them with you and can use them for growth and transformation.

Because we can hold onto grievances a little extra longer during Scorpio Season, Rhodonite can help you let go and learn from your experience.

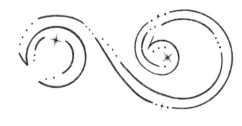

 Affirmations

I am getting to the bottom of things.

My power is in the darkness.

I will transform and rise again.

 *Journal Prompts*

What in your life is out of balance?

_____

_____

_____

What can you do to help correct that balance?

_____

_____

_____

What relationship needs tending now?

_____

_____

_____

Scorpio Season Horoscopes

Aries
This is a time of profound transformation, as the sun highlights your sense of personal power. The next month is great for therapy shadow work, and anything that helps clear the cobwebs out of the mental closet.

Taurus
You'll find your power by joining with others now, both in personal and professional life. Cultivate a sense of partnership in your relationships and be open about voicing your needs.

Gemini
The stars give you the green light to shake up your daily routine and put some nourishing practices in place. Attention to your habits now sets the foundation for your future growth in all areas of your life.

Cancer
You now want to stretch your legs and express yourself after sticking close to home and nesting. Creative adventures take precedence now, and you're encouraged to follow your spontaneity when it comes to playing, pleasure, and creativity.

Leo
Your focus turns to your home and family and creating a safe, nurturing nest to retreat to. You desire to put down roots and feel a sense of belonging. Now is a time to go inward and nourish yourself.

Virgo
This is a time perfect for making new connections, connecting with old friends, networking, and collaborating with others. Speaking up and using your voice has a stronger impact now, and you share your message with ease.

Libra
This is when you are focused on security, what helps you feel safe and comfortable, and what you value. If you set your mind to making a financial plan for the year ahead, you might find that it pays off later.

Scorpio
You're gaining a clearer understanding of who you are as the Sun illuminates your inner rebirth. This clarity helps you take spontaneous action towards the new and exciting to carve out your path forward.

Sagittarius
You may feel like retreating from the world and spending time alone now. Use this time to reflect on the year past, dream of the year ahead, and refill your energetic cup.

Capricorn
Your focus is shifting to your community and friends. Groups and gatherings are important to you now, and you're feeling social and lighthearted.

Aquarius
Now is the best time of the year to move forward in your career. Recognition and responsibility go hand in hand as the Sun illuminates this part of your chart.

Pisces
Adventure calls your name as you seek new experiences and more meaning in your life. Travel, education, learning new hobbies, and exploring your spirituality all attract your attention.

Scorpio Season Journal

What did I learn this season?

_____

_____

_____

What am I still learning?

_____

_____

_____

What am I releasing?

_____

_____

_____

_____

_____

What do I intend for next season?

_____

_____

_____

Any other thoughts, dreams, or desires you wish to note:

_____

_____

_____

_____

_____

_____

_____

_____

_____

_____

_____

_____

_____

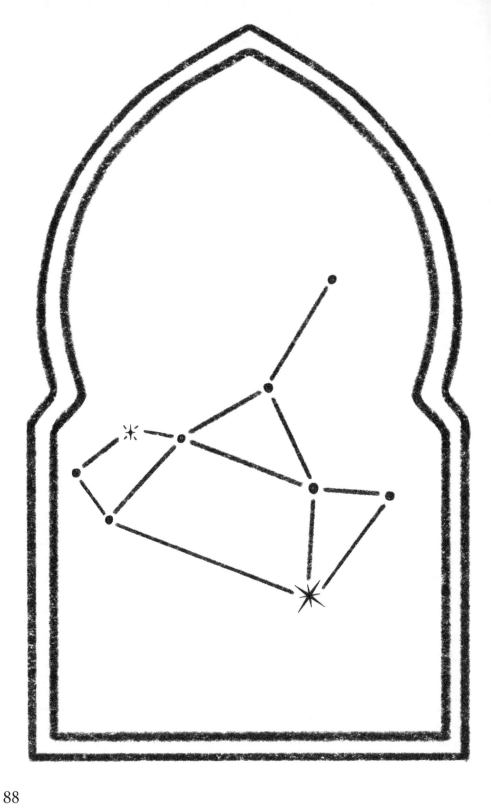

SAGITTARIUS

With Sagittarius, the focus is on looking to the future with an optimistic outlook and expanding your horizons through learning, travel, adventure, and spirituality. Sagittarius is ruled by Jupiter, the planet of expansion, abundance, and growth. While on the surface, Sagittarius energy wants to explore, travel, and seek out adventures, there is a more profound need and desire to turn that wanderlust energy inward through higher education, spirituality, and gathering wisdom. Balanced Sagittarius energy has equal outward expansion and inward knowing and intuition.

Sagittarius Correspondences

House	Element	Quality	Planetary Ruler
9th	Fire	Mutable	Jupiter

Season	Body Part
Autumn	Hips, thighs

Sagittarius Season Energy

For Sagittarius Season, our focus shifts to looking to our future with an optimistic outlook and expanding our horizons through learning, travel, adventure, and spirituality. Sagittarius is the last of the fire signs in the zodiac and is the sign that heralds the end of Autumn. At this point in the season, we've finished up the bulk of our metaphorical harvest from the seeds we've sown over the year and are looking forward to gathering with friends and family to celebrate.

IN BALANCE	OUT OF BALANCE
Adventurous	Risks too much
Loves to learn	Overconfident
Independent	Resists commitment
Risk-taker	Restless
Optimist	Dogmatic
Inspirational	Blunt
Spiritual	Exaggerates
Confident	Reacts to boundaries
Honest	Careless

Soul Care Tools

The symbol of Sagittarius is that of a Centaur, a creature that is half horse and half man. Sagittarius represents the line between our two minds. Our more base, animal instincts mind seeks out knowledge and higher understanding. During Sagittarius Season, we seek to find the balance between our quest for knowledge and learning while also having a place to return to and nourish our roots.

Body Awareness

Sagittarius rules the hips and thighs, including the muscles and bones of these areas. That is why movement is essential to this sign and all of us when we're in Sagittarius Season. Because Sagittarius is all about wandering, traveling, and exploring, walking or hiking is an excellent form of both exercise and self-care.

Herbs

The herbal allies for Sagittarius help keep this energy in balance. If you find yourself struggling to embody the confident Sagittarius fire, you may want to include some warming herbs into your diet or through herbal tea (ginger is a personal favorite). Or if you find yourself a little too hot under the collar and need to slow down that reckless impulse, try some yarrow or nettles.

Gemstones

Gemstones are another great way to connect to the energy of the season. Blue Lace Agate helps you connect with your innate and inner wisdom while keeping you in touch with your emotions. This is key during Sagittarius Season when we can look outward for insight and spiritual guidance instead of looking inside ourselves.

Wonderful for clearing and releasing old patterns and energy that no longer serves us, Sodalite is helpful for encouraging intuitive abilities and helping us get to the root of inner struggles.

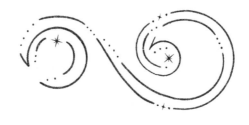 Affirmations

I am bringing my dreams to reality.

I brave the adventure of life.

I take aim at my goals.

 Journal Prompts

What will help me take aim at my dreams?

_____

_____

_____

What in my life needs to expand?

_____

_____

_____

How can I trust in the Universe more?

_____

_____

_____

Sagittarius Season Horoscopes

Aries
Adventure calls your name as you seek new experiences and more meaning in your life. Travel, education, learning new hobbies, and exploring your spirituality all attract your attention.

Taurus
This is a time of profound transformation, as the sun highlights your sense of personal power. The next month is great for therapy shadow work, and anything that helps clear the cobwebs out of the mental closet.

Gemini
You'll find your power by joining with others now, both in personal and professional life. Cultivate a sense of partnership in your relationships and be open about voicing your needs.

Cancer
The stars give you the green light to shake up your daily routine and put some nourishing practices in place. Attention to your habits now sets the foundation for your future growth in all areas of your life.

Leo
You now want to stretch your legs and express yourself after sticking close to home and nesting. Creative adventures take precedence now, and you're encouraged to follow your spontaneity when it comes to playing, pleasure, and creativity.

Virgo
Your focus turns to your home and family and creating a safe, nurturing nest to retreat to. You desire to put down roots and feel a sense of belonging. Now is a time to go inward and nourish yourself.

Libra
This is a time perfect for making new connections, connecting with old friends, networking, and collaborating with others. Speaking up and using your voice has a stronger impact now, and you share your

message with ease. # Scorpio
This is when you are focused on security, what helps you feel safe and comfortable, and what you value. If you set your mind to making a financial plan for the year ahead, you might find that it pays off later.

Sagittarius
You're gaining a clearer understanding of who you are as the Sun illuminates your inner rebirth. This clarity helps you take spontaneous action towards the new and exciting to carve out your path forward.

Capricorn
You may feel like retreating from the world and spending time alone now. Use this time to reflect on the year past, dream of the year ahead, and refill your energetic cup.

Aquarius
Your focus is shifting to your community and friends. Groups and gatherings are important to you now, and you're feeling social and lighthearted.

Pisces
Now is the best time of the year to move forward in your career. Recognition and responsibility go hand in hand as the Sun illuminates this part of your chart.

Sagittarius Season Journal

What did I learn this season?

_____

_____

_____

What am I still learning?

_____

_____

_____

What am I releasing?

_____

_____

_____

_____

_____

What do I intend for next season?

_____

_____

_____

Any other thoughts, dreams, or desires you wish to note:

_____

_____

_____

_____

_____

_____

_____

_____

_____

_____

_____

_____

_____

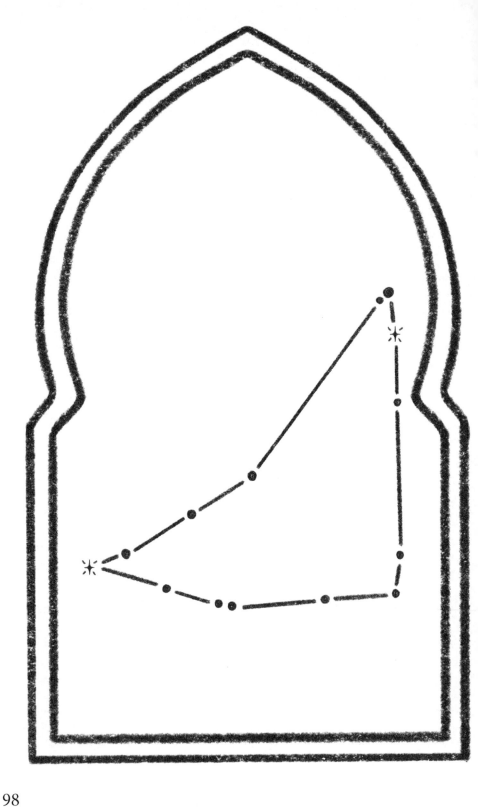

CAPRICORN

Capricorn has a laser focus on its goals and seeks to put its mastery towards climbing and making progress that impacts others. Capricorn is a sea-goat, a half-goat, half-fish animal. The head and upper half are a goat, where the lower half looks like a fish or mermaid tail. Capricorn is seen as ambitious, wanting to climb its goal mountain no matter what rock slides or boulders are in the way. Ruled by Saturn, the planet of discipline, time, and responsibility, Capricorn has no qualms about hunkering down to get things done. They know how to use their time efficiently and create order out of chaos.

Capricorn Correspondences

House	Element	Quality	Planetary Ruler
10th	Earth	Cardinal	Saturn

	Season		Body Part
	Winter		Skeletal system

Capricorn Season Energy

For Capricorn Season, our focus shifts to long-term visions, dreams, and plans. Capricorn is the cardinal earth sign, marking the beginning of Winter in the Northern Hemisphere. We're saying goodbye to the year ending, reviewing and taking stock of our accomplishments, and setting our sights on newer and brighter goals for the year ahead. It is a season of hope and possibility, and courage and faith that we can do the work needed to get to where we want to go.

IN BALANCE	OUT OF BALANCE
Responsible	Hides emotions
Grounded	Fearful
Disciplined	Depressed
Ambitious	Pessimistic
Practical	Rigid
Structured	Cold
Persistent	Proud
Conservative	Workaholic

Soul Care Tools

Capricorn is known in the zodiac space as being ambitious and ready to take on the world to climb its mountain. But we have to remember what inspired us to have those goals in the first place. So it's important during Capricorn Season to name your goals and write them down and pay attention to the feelings that arise within you as you look at your goals. Your goals are your sacred calling, your soul's purpose.

Body Awareness

Capricorn rules the bones, so keeping your joints in top shape is vital. You may find yourself craving snacks that you can sink your teeth into, which has a bit of a crunch. Make sure you're moving your body to keep your muscles tension free and give your bones room to move.

Herbs

The herbal allies for Capricorn help remind us that we are more than our goals and to-do lists. We are physical beings with needs that must be met to do more than survive but thrive. Rosemary helps us remember this and allows us to relax our focus into more pleasurable pursuits. Ginger is also another excellent herb for this time of year, as it is warming, and also can help reduce inflammation that can cause joint pain, an area of the body ruled by Capricorn.

Gemstones

Gemstones are another great way to connect to the energy of the season. One of the gems associated with Capricorn Season, Garnet, emphasizes strength, dependability, and commitment.

If you find yourself becoming too rigid in your thinking during Capricorn Season, try using Green Calcite, as it helps to lessen rigid thinking and belief structures.

While Capricorn energy is steadfast and hardworking, the energy can make us feel a little too grounded and perhaps melancholy. Pyrite helps lift us up and instill confidence.

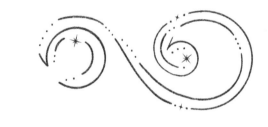

 Affirmations

I am reaching the top of my mountain.

I can be strong and tender.

I am determined to reach my goal.

# Journal Prompts

What area of my life needs more structure and routine?

_____

_____

_____

What will help me further my goals?

_____

_____

_____

How can I be less rigid in my approach?

_____

_____

_____

Capricorn Season Horoscopes

Aries
Now is the best time of the year to move forward in your career. Recognition and responsibility go hand in hand as the Sun illuminates this part of your chart.

Taurus
Adventure calls your name as you seek new experiences and more meaning in your life. Travel, education, learning new hobbies, and exploring your spirituality all attract your attention.

Gemini
This is a time of profound transformation, as the sun highlights your sense of personal power. The next month is great for therapy shadow work, and anything that helps clear the cobwebs out of the mental closet.

Cancer
You'll find your power by joining with others now, both in personal and professional life. Cultivate a sense of partnership in your relationships and be open about voicing your needs.

Leo
The stars give you the green light to shake up your daily routine and put some nourishing practices in place. Attention to your habits now sets the foundation for your future growth in all areas of your life.

Virgo
You now want to stretch your legs and express yourself after sticking close to home and nesting. Creative adventures take precedence now, and you're encouraged to follow your spontaneity when it comes to playing, pleasure, and creativity.

Libra
Your focus turns to your home and family and creating a safe, nurturing nest to retreat to. You desire to put down roots and feel a sense of belonging. Now is a time to go inward and nourish yourself.

Scorpio
This is a time perfect for making new connections, connecting with old friends, networking, and collaborating with others. Speaking up and using your voice has a stronger impact now, and you share your message with ease.

Sagittarius
This is when you are focused on security, what helps you feel safe and comfortable, and what you value. If you set your mind to making a financial plan for the year ahead, you might find that it pays off later.

Capricorn
You're gaining a clearer understanding of who you are as the Sun illuminates your inner rebirth. This clarity helps you take spontaneous action towards the new and exciting to carve out your path forward.

Aquarius
You may feel like retreating from the world and spending time alone now. Use this time to reflect on the year past, dream of the year ahead, and refill your energetic cup.

Pisces
Your focus is shifting to your community and friends. Groups and gatherings are important to you now, and you're feeling social and lighthearted.

Capricorn Season Journal

What did I learn this season?

_____

_____

_____

What am I still learning?

_____

_____

_____

What am I releasing?

_____

_____

_____

_____

_____

What do I intend for next season?

_____

_____

_____

Any other thoughts, dreams, or desires you wish to note:

_____

_____

_____

_____

_____

_____

_____

_____

_____

_____

_____

_____

_____

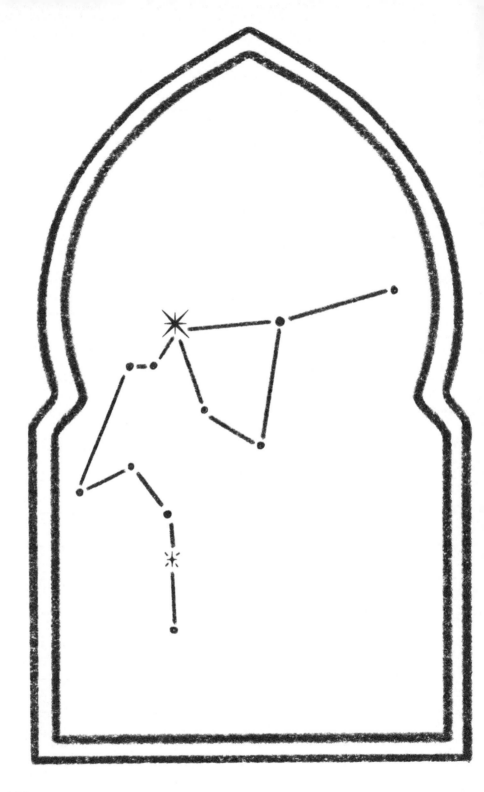

AQUARIUS

Aquarius is often described as the black sheep of the zodiac. Unpredictable, this sign lives for innovation and is constantly trying new methods and testing them out. As an air sign, Aquarius very much can get lost in their mental world, and because of this, they can have sensitive nervous systems. When the needs of the physical body are cast aside for the mind to work with the inspiration at hand, insomnia can creep in, as well as becoming emotionally detached and rebelling for the sake of it. Ruled by Uranus, the planet of revolution and rebellion, Aquarius doesn't do well being put into a box and craves to strike out on their own and be themselves.

Aquarius Correspondences

House	Element	Quality	Planetary Ruler
11th	Air	Fixed	Uranus, Saturn

Season	Body Part
Winter	Circulatory system

 # Aquarius Season Energy

For Aquarius Season, our focus shifts to long-term visions, dreams, and plans. Aquarius is the fixed air sign, right in the middle of Winter in the Northern Hemisphere. But even though fixed signs have a reputation for being stubborn, Aquarius is also unpredictable. This sign lives for innovation and invention and is constantly trying new methods and testing them out.

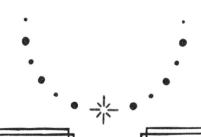

IN BALANCE	OUT OF BALANCE
Community-oriented	Detached
Visionary	Rebellious
Progressive	Aloof
Innovative	Impractical
Science-minded	Unreliable
Independent	Zealous
Insightful	Stubborn
Enlightened	Disruptive
Inspirational	Avoids commitment

Soul Care Tools

As an air sign, Aquarius very much can get lost in their mental world, and because of this, they can have sensitive nervous systems. When the needs of the physical body are cast aside for the mind to work with the inspiration at hand, insomnia can creep in, and we become emotionally detached and rebelling for the sake of it.

Body Awareness

Aquarius rules the circulatory system, the blood, and energy that moves through your body. A key for Aquarius is moving the body to keep the blood moving, so energy doesn't get stuck and stagnant. How can you get your body moving? What new routine do you want to try? How can you think outside of the box for going about your self-care and tending to your needs? Diving into these questions is where we'll find the answers we seek during the Aquarius season.

Herbs

The herbal allies for Aquarius Season relax the body and mind, boosting our sense of compassion. Valerian is one such herb and can improve sleep quality and reduce anxiety when consumed as tea before bed. Hawthorn is another Aquarius herb that is a powerful circulatory system aid but try Rose Hips if you're looking for something a little gentler. Rose Hips contain Vitamin C, and studies have shown that Rose Hips may boost heath health by reducing blood pressure and lowering cholesterol.

Gemstones

Gemstones are another great way to connect to the energy of the season. Intimacy can be difficult during Aquarius Season, as this air sign is more comfortable in the realm of facts than emotions. Relationships can feel cold and distant now, but you can bring warmth and comfort to your relationship with Rose Quartz.

Blue Celestite helps to amplify the positive qualities of Aquarius Season, such as helping fellow humans and looking to make change for the good of everyone.

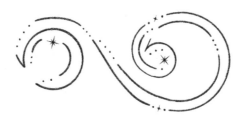

I innovate for a better world.

I celebrate my differences.

Together we evolve.

 *Journal Prompts*

How can I use my gifts and talents to help others?

_____

_____

_____

Have I become too detached from my emotions?

_____

_____

_____

How can I feel more connected to others?

_____

_____

_____

Aquarius Season Horoscopes

Aries
Your focus is shifting to your community and friends. Groups and gatherings are important to you now, and you're feeling social and lighthearted.

Taurus
Now is the best time of the year to move forward in your career. Recognition and responsibility go hand in hand as the Sun illuminates this part of your chart.

Gemini
Adventure calls your name as you seek new experiences and more meaning in your life. Travel, education, learning new hobbies, and exploring your spirituality all attract your attention.

Cancer
This is a time of profound transformation, as the sun highlights your sense of personal power. The next month is great for therapy shadow work, and anything that helps clear the cobwebs out of the mental closet.

Leo
You'll find your power by joining with others now, both in personal and professional life. Cultivate a sense of partnership in your relationships and be open about voicing your needs.

Virgo

The stars give you the green light to shake up your daily routine and put some nourishing practices in place. Attention to your habits now sets the foundation for your future growth in all areas of your life.

Libra

You now want to stretch your legs and express yourself after sticking close to home and nesting. Creative adventures take precedence now, and you're encouraged to follow your spontaneity when it comes to playing, pleasure, and creativity.

Scorpio

Your focus turns to your home and family and creating a safe, nurturing nest to retreat to. You desire to put down roots and feel a sense of belonging. Now is a time to go inward and nourish yourself.

Sagittarius

This is a time perfect for making new connections, connecting with old friends, networking, and collaborating with others. Speaking up and using your voice has a stronger impact now, and you share your message with ease.

Capricorn

This is when you are focused on security, what helps you feel safe and comfortable, and what you value. If you set your mind to making a financial plan for the year ahead, you might find that it pays off later.

Aquarius

You're gaining a clearer understanding of who you are as the Sun illuminates your inner rebirth. This clarity helps you take spontaneous action towards the new and exciting to carve out your path forward.

Pisces

You may feel like retreating from the world and spending time alone now. Use this time to reflect on the year past, dream of the year ahead, and refill your energetic cup.

Aquarius Season Journal

What did I learn this season?

_____

_____

_____

What am I still learning?

_____

_____

_____

What am I releasing?

_____

_____

_____

_____

_____

_____

What do I intend for next season?

_____

_____

_____

Any other thoughts, dreams, or desires you wish to note:

_____

_____

_____

_____

_____

_____

_____

_____

_____

_____

_____

_____

_____

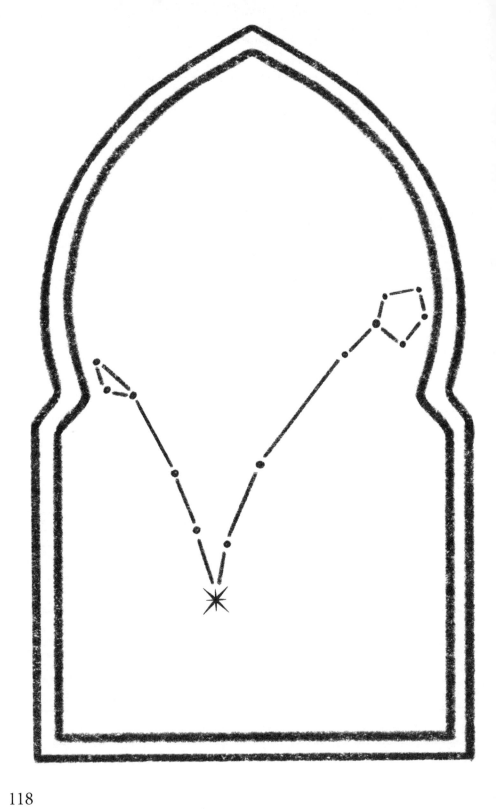

118

PISCES

Pisces is the dreamer of the zodiac. With Pisces, we're holding the line between the dream work and reality, striving to find the middle ground that will serve us. If we keep our heads stuck in the clouds too long, we can lose our grip on reality, becoming caught up in daydreams, illusions, and fantasies. On the other hand, if we don't let ourselves dream and stay out of touch with that part of ourselves, we can become passive-aggressive and let life pass us by instead of actively engaging in it. Ruled by Neptune, the planet of dreams and illusions, Pisces straddles the line between this world and the next and can bring the images of our imagination to life with unmatched creativity.

Pisces Correspondences

House	Element	Quality	Planetary Ruler
12th	Water	Mutable	Jupiter, Neptune

Season	Body Part
Winter	Feet, lymphatic system

Pisces Season Energy

For Pisces Season, our focus seems to expand to everyone and no-where at the same time. We feel inspired and have many creative ideas, but it can be hard to focus and ground to turn these ideas into reality. Pisces is the mutable water sign that heralds the transition into Spring (the mutable signs mark the ending of one season and the beginning of the next). Mutable signs are more flexible and adaptable, straddling the lines between elements.

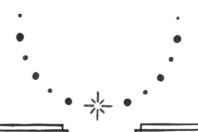

IN BALANCE	OUT OF BALANCE
Sensitive	Escapist
Intuitive	Deceptive
Spiritual	Avoidance of reality
Mystic	Stuck in fantasy
Compassionate	Ungrounded
Romantic	Shy
Inspired	Addictions
Imaginative	Procrastinate
Enchanting	Boundary issues
Soulful	Vulnerable

# Soul Care Tools

With Pisces, we're holding the line between the dream work and reality, striving to find the middle ground that will serve us. If we keep our heads stuck in the clouds too long, we can lose our grip on reality, becoming caught up in daydreams, illusions, and fantasies. On the other hand, if we don't let ourselves dream and stay out of touch with that part of ourselves, we can become passive-aggressive and let life pass us by instead of actively engaging in it.

Body Awareness

We need to cultivate a relationship with ourselves through time alone to explore our dreams. This can be done with music, meditation, spending time in nature, or working with your creativity in a 'non-productive' way, a way in which you have no goal but are just there to explore and be curious. Pisces rules the feet, so it's essential to use this connection to stay grounded to the earth no matter how high our mind tries to travel up in the clouds. Foot massages and exercises where you activate all the different parts of your feet can help with this.

Herbs

The herbal allies for Pisces help us ease into our dreams and float away. You can create a wonderful foot soak with epsom salt and a few soothing herbs, such as lavender, eucalyptus, chamomile, and lemon balm. Mugwort is an herb that is said to aid in lucid dreaming and astral projection when massaged between the eyebrows before bedtime.

Gemstones

Gemstones are another great way to connect to the energy of the season. Helping to keep us strong in our own identity, Chrysoprase helps to break co-dependency, as well as form a bridge connection to the divine and inspiration.

During Pisces Season, we can feel very sensitive, as well as intuitive. Amethyst helps calm those sensitive waters and keep your energy clear. It's also great for blocking negative energy, as well as tapping into your intuition.

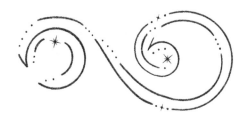

I see the spiritual in the mundane.

I celebrate my feelings.

My sensitivity is my superpower.

Journal Prompts

What can my dreams reveal to me?

_____

_____

_____

What area of my life could use more creativity?

_____

_____

_____

How can I nourish my dreams?

_____

_____

_____

Pisces Season Horoscopes

Aries
You may feel like retreating from the world and spending time alone now. Use this time to reflect on the year past, dream of the year ahead, and refill your energetic cup.

Taurus
Your focus is shifting to your community and friends. Groups and gatherings are important to you now, and you're feeling social and lighthearted.

Gemini
Now is the best time of the year to move forward in your career. Recognition and responsibility go hand in hand as the Sun illuminates this part of your chart.

Cancer
Adventure calls your name as you seek new experiences and more meaning in your life. Travel, education, learning new hobbies, and exploring your spirituality all attract your attention.

Leo
This is a time of profound transformation, as the sun highlights your sense of personal power. The next month is great for therapy shadow work, and anything that helps clear the cobwebs out of the mental closet.

Virgo
You'll find your power by joining with others now, both in personal and professional life. Cultivate a sense of partnership in your relationships and be open about voicing your needs.

Libra
The stars give you the green light to shake up your daily routine and put some nourishing practices in place. Attention to your habits now sets the foundation for your future growth in all areas of your life.

Scorpio
You now want to stretch your legs and express yourself after sticking close to home and nesting. Creative adventures take precedence now, and you're encouraged to follow your spontaneity when it comes to playing, pleasure, and creativity.

Sagittarius
Your focus turns to your home and family and creating a safe, nurturing nest to retreat to. You desire to put down roots and feel a sense of belonging. Now is a time to go inward and nourish yourself.

Capricorn
This is a time perfect for making new connections, connecting with old friends, networking, and collaborating with others. Speaking up and using your voice has a stronger impact now, and you share your message with ease.

Aquarius
This is when you are focused on security, what helps you feel safe and comfortable, and what you value. If you set your mind to making a financial plan for the year ahead, you might find that it pays off later.

Pisces
You're gaining a clearer understanding of who you are as the Sun illuminates your inner rebirth. This clarity helps you take spontaneous action towards the new and exciting to carve out your path forward.

Pisces Season Journal

What did I learn this season?

_____

_____

_____

What am I still learning?

_____

_____

_____

_____

What am I releasing?

_____

_____

_____

_____

_____

_____

What do I intend for next season?

_____

_____

_____

Any other thoughts, dreams, or desires you wish to note:

_____

_____

_____

_____

_____

_____

_____

_____

_____

_____

_____

_____

_____

ABOUT THE AUTHOR

Sara McCormick is an astrologer and writer based in North Carolina. When she's not dreaming, writing, or gazing at the moon, Sara can be found working in her garden, playing with her son and trying to convince her husband that they have room for just one more cat.

Follow her on Social Media
Twitter @soulcareastro
Facebook @soulcareastrology
Instagram @soulcareastrology

You can find more of her work on her website.

www.soulcareastrology.com

Printed in Great Britain
by Amazon